FAMOUS

What He Bought Is So Much
Better Than What You Can Build

Tommy Miller

Sermon To Book
www.sermontobook.com

Famous Church / Tommy Miller
ISBN-13: 9780692501511
ISBN-10: 0692501517

This book is dedicated to Shanda. My wife, best friend, soul mate, and inspiration—Shanda Miller. No one in the world has taught me more about the heart of God and the unconditional love of Jesus than my bride. Thank you, Shanda, for believing. You are perfect, and I love you unconditionally, forever, and always.

CONTENTS

Foreword

Tommy Miller's knowledge of the Scriptures and his heart to unveil the bride of Christ are brought to life in *Famous Church.* I find his teaching on this subject to be, frankly, a breathe of fresh air. For many years I have searched to find those in the church who believe what the Scriptures say about the Father wanting to pour out His glory on His bride so the world would have to stop, look, and listen.

Famous Church uncovers the truth that we have had false humility and have been tricked into thinking it is ungodly and prideful to believe our Father would give His best for us, His purified and perfected bride.

I love the boldness in this book, and I believe it will serve to compel the church no longer to put up with religious traditions that desire to keep us beaten down, worried, and unsuccessful. "The world is unimpressed with a church who is schizophrenic in its belief of who she is." The Father God's heart speaks through Tommy in *Famous Church* and shows that it's time we start walking, talking, and being the bride that Jesus adores every day, not just on Sunday!

Bill Ballenger

National Recording Artist and Founder of Break the Grey, Inc.

CHAPTER ONE

Making God Famous

"My bride doesn't know how to abound."

This was the statement that God clearly put on my heart while driving to a guest speaking engagement in Louisville, Ohio. It was one of those moments that make you gasp, cringe, and sigh in relief all at once. The more I pondered and researched, the more I saw that this was oh, so true!

In Philippians 4:12, Paul says, "I have learned to be *abased*" (NKJV), which means to be brought low. Then it says that Paul learned how to *abound.* The Strong's Concordance defines "abound" as to be "furnished so liberally" that we overflow and want for nothing—to be *great*! The church is called to be the visible representation of the most excellent man who ever stepped into time, and who is above all things.

I'm starting to think we may have missed our call to be excellent. Why? I know there are quite a few areas of mediocrity in my own life. As you read, I pray that you examine yourself to see if you find the same. Could it be that the way we interpret Scripture can, at times, encourage mediocrity? Might our internal religious conditioning take over and prohibit ourselves from thinking rightly about ourselves out of fear of pride? Might we actually neglect to see the fullness of what God promises to and desires for His church?

> *For whoever exalts himself will be humbled, and he who humbles himself will be exalted.* — **Luke 14:11, NKJV**

I've heard plenty of sermons tell Christians that they are not worthy to receive honor of any type, but I have yet to hear many teachings on this passage in its proper context. Look at the verse that directly precedes it:

> *But when you are invited, go and sit down in the lowest place, so that when he who invited you comes he may say to you, "Friend, go up higher." Then you will have glory in the presence of those who sit at the table with you.* — **Luke 14:10, NKJV**

These passages do more than just guarantee that if we wrongfully exalt ourselves, we'll have the rug pulled out from under us. They also promise that when we rightly and humbly come to God, we'll be famous! Paul knew how to be famous in God yet humble in himself. That is what learning how to abound truly is. If we humble ourselves, there is a certainty according to the Word of God that we will be given prestige and the opportunity to magnify Jesus for who *He* is.

So let's spare the religious conditioning, false humility, and self-righteousness. You know you all want to be great, anyway! That's the way God wired you. Look at Genesis: you are *supposed* to subdue all things. Now let's take another look at this verse:

> *For whoever exalts himself will be humbled, and he who humbles himself will be exalted.* — ***Luke 14:11, NKJV***

The Strong's Concordance defines "exalt" as "to raise to the very summit of opulence and prosperity, to exalt, to raise to dignity, honor and happiness." Herein lies a guarantee that we will have to learn in order to part of the famous church we are called to be. In verse 10 we are commanded to "go up higher" after humbling ourselves, with the promise that we will have the glory of those who sit at the big table.

The Greek word *doxa* is the word that translates to our English word "glory" (translated "worship" in the King James translation of the Bible). It is defined by Strong's Concordance as "the kingly majesty which belongs to him as supreme ruler, majesty in the sense of the absolute perfection of the deity, the absolutely perfect inward or personal excellency of Christ; the majesty." We now, as His bride, carry His wealth, His dignity, His glory, and His excellence. Why? Because He chose us and we said, "I do."

This story bears a striking resemblance to the plotline of *Pretty Woman*, starring Richard Gere and Julia Roberts. Vivian (Roberts) is a prostitute on Hollywood

Boulevard when Edward Lewis (Gere) comes to town. What starts out as a business deal ends up turning into a relationship. However, the trouble comes when Vivian starts to be introduced into Edward's world of wealth, prestige, and greatness. If you've seen the movie, you remember the scene where Edwards gives her full access to his credit cards to go shopping at one of the fanciest places on Rodeo drive. She walks in fully equipped to buy the entire store, yet leaves with only one dress because she sees herself through the eyes of the shop clerk as unworthy.

This is often the same road that we take as the church. We are used to living by the law (a "you get what you deserve" mentality) and have such a hard time receiving something we didn't earn (the wealth, greatness, and prestige of our new lover). We listen to the opinions and reactions of people around us to determine our value, identity, and ability instead of to the one who owns us, who paid the price for us, determining our value and giving us His identity.

Please continue to read with an open mind and an eager heart. We are a city on a hill that is to be seen from far away. May God meet you in the pages of this writing, lifting you to the next levels of glory and faith that He has for you.

CHAPTER TWO

The Call to Excellence

So the LORD was with Joshua, and his fame spread throughout the land. —***Joshua 6:27, NIV***

Sometimes churches seem to have professionals on one side of the stage and spectators on the other. But the apostle Paul was very clear in 1 Corinthians 12 and in the book of Romans on His design for His church: what He bought is so much better than what we can build. There was never a concept of "us" and "them." The Bible says man was made in God's image. God is a triune God—three persons but One God—and no one person of the Trinity is any less important or less powerful than the other.

When God made man in His image, He intended for the Body, the church, to reflect that image. God's people were to be coequal and have the same value, but different roles. A pastor is no more important than the servant cleaning the toilets. As a matter of fact, according to the Word, God bestows greater honor on those whom we see as less important. They were *all* meant to reflect Him and His fame.

The church was never meant to be an entity that hid in the cracks and crevices. It was never supposed to be something people only heard about when they were invited to a service. It was meant to be visible, to make a difference in the community, to be powerful, and to be famous.

The church described in Scripture has so much wealth and so much power that if it were to become a reality today, when things like city roads need repair, the city would come to the church for help because we have a resource that never runs out. When somebody becomes sick, the first place they think of should not be the doctor; it should be the church. The church was given authority over all material things.

Consider This Testimony

Consider what Scripture says about me, about you, about *us*. If I were to share my testimony with you, it would sound just like this:

"I'm the wealthiest man on the planet, and my Father is richer than everybody else. Nobody has any say over anything that I do. Sickness can't tell me what to do; I've been given authority and dominion over everything.

"I, (your name here), have been given authority and dominion over all things. I'm so rich, my resources can never run out. The Creator of this universe loves me so much that He died for me, giving everything He had because He thinks I'm worth it. He gave His life for me. Every area of my life I've fallen short in has been forever erased; I have a clean slate. I'm perfect."

I admit this sounds arrogant and pompous, but truly, this is what the Scriptures say about me and you as God's children.

Why Is It So Much Easier for People to Say They Are Broken?

Why then is it easier for us, God's chosen children, to hide in our brokenness, playing church and waiting until the clouds split and Jesus comes back to take us home, as if we were "barely saved," anyway? I don't know about you, but that's not what my Bible says. As a son of the Creator of the universe, living in this world, I'm here to make some noise—to take what God has freely given me and turn the world upside down. My Bible says that nothing can touch me and that I have been blessed with every spiritual blessing in the heavenly realm.

Know this: *excellence is not pride, and laziness is not humility!*

Look in the book of Exodus, for example. The Hebrews escaped Egypt, where they had been held captive as slaves under Pharaoh for 400 years. In the Bible, Egypt is a picture of our past. It is a picture of the Christian being stuck in a place of shame, bondage and despair. God brought this entire nation into a place of freedom, every need of theirs was met, food was falling from heaven, and their clothes never wore out; but in spite of this, they still acted like they were slaves. They refused to believe the promise because, let's face it, after living that way for so long, the promise seemed too good to be true!

Why is it so hard to believe that God's intent is that the church is supposed to be famous? Why is it so hard for us to receive? As Christians we tend to partake in the most ignorant of escapades, in which we think we are better than each other based on how little we think of ourselves. This is the absolute epitome of self-righteousness and ultimately the demise of the Famous Church. Again, know this: *excellence is not pride, and laziness is not humility!* We shame each other for being noticed, for gaining audience, and for putting God on display, leaving all of us so terrified of the opinions of religious people that we would prefer to shrink back and hide to appease them, rather than be the city on a hill as we've been called to be.

Did you ever wonder why there is a burning desire in you for greatness but, along with that, there is a perceived shame in its pursuit? Allow me to explain. God wired you to be just like He is. The first commandments you received were to "be fruitful and multiply; fill the earth and subdue it" (Genesis 1:28, NKJV). That, my friends, is a call to excellence.

Within each one of us, there is an innate need to be our created self, the one God designed. Over time, the pursuit of greatness, or living it out in our lives, has been shamed. Christians pride themselves in being "humble," but their understanding of the term is wrong. Humility is not placing a low value on yourself; it's placing low importance, and giving credit where it is due, to the One who created you. When the need to be great is mixed with the suppression of the desire to be great because we are trying to appease people, it results in this "itch that can't be scratched" type of lifestyle in which, as soon as you start to abound, you cause yourself to be abased because you don't recognize that it is God who is prospering you. This is why we feel the way we feel when it comes to our pursuit of greatness, being fruitful, multiplying, filling the earth, and bringing it under subjection.

When an animal contracts rabies, one of the symptoms is *hydrophobia*, or a fear of water. The animal was created to drink, but its mind is telling it that water is evil. The closer it gets to water, the harder it pushes itself away, which is actually where the foaming at the mouth comes from.

The promise the Israelites received was a good promise. The Promised Land was a good land, a land flowing with milk and honey. But it was also full of giants. All Israel had to do was trust God and go into the land; God would drive the giants out. This second generation of Israelites who trusted God and lived to enter the land saw God miraculously drive out Israel's enemies.

Today I have rolled away the reproach of Egypt from you." — ***Joshua 5:9, NIV***

God took away the reproach of Israel's past, and He does the same for you and me. You have been made new in Christ. Sometimes it's hard not to ask questions about God's involvement in the world when there are so many terrible things going on. Why do innocent children go through unspeakable atrocities? Why are the Iraqis and the Syrians fighting? Why is terrorism so rampant?

In Ephesians 2, Paul declares that God raised Jesus high above every principality, power, and dominion. He placed everything under Jesus's feet, and then Jesus gave authority in all things over to the church. God delegated. He gave people both the ability and the responsibility to harness His power over all things for the purpose of making Him famous.

There is a turning point happening, a pendulum swing if you will, in the church today. God is revealing to the church the truth of what it's called to be. It is starting in individual churches, and it will spread around the globe. It's profoundly important to remember this, when difficult things happen and people ask, "*Why would you let this happen, God*?"

God is answering, "I delegated."

Making God Famous

God's presence was with Joshua as he courageously led the Israelites into the Promised Land. Joshua 6:7 says, "So the LORD was with Joshua, and his fame spread throughout the land" (NIV). What God was doing through one obedient man caused the entire country to turn their attention toward what Joshua was doing. God's fame (or reputation) spread throughout the country.

Sometimes we think we need to portray godly "humility" to others, and we do this by staying in the shadows. We think this will give God all the glory. But that's not what happened in the Scriptures. God used weak men all the time to accomplish what He wanted. These men were passionate about seeing God's will fulfilled on the earth.

We can't see what we have faith in, but when we act, the world can see our faith.

Are we? Do we say, as Isaiah said to God, "Here am I. Send me!" (Isaiah 6:8, NKJV)? Isaiah's answer was personal, not communal. He said that he himself—not his church, not his denomination—would represent God. God is looking for those whom He can put in the spotlight, but who will point to where their power comes from.

The apostle Paul understood this. As he saw the gospel spreading across the known world of the time, he wrote: "First, I thank my God through Jesus Christ for you all, that your faith is spoken of *throughout the whole world"* (Romans 1:8, KJV).

Paul knew these early believers were doing some amazing things, but he thanked God through Jesus Christ for the faith of those boldly sharing the gospel.

The book of James sheds the brightest light in all of theology on things concerning faith. It is painfully clear in saying that faith is dead, literally translated "destitute of life," without works. Nobody is going to know about the faith you have if you keep it tucked away in your heart. You must display it to world. We can't see whom or what we have faith in, but the world can see that we have faith.

The Word of God says you are made in His image. You should be like a magnifying glass that people see Christ through. To accomplish this Christ-like glow, He paid to make you shine.

Yet, at the same time, being a Christian does not mean being the center of attention. It isn't about being a prima donna. This is about simply being who God called His people to be. It's impossible to follow Jesus passionately and not have your life become a big deal.

In John 17, when Jesus spoke these words, He lifted up His eyes to heaven and said: "Father, the hour has come. Glorify your Son, that your Son may glorify you" (John 17:1, NIV).

This is a pretty brave prayer. Jesus was saying, "Make Me a big deal, so I can make You a big deal." And Jesus prayed this with a pure heart and a pure conscious.

Can that be our prayer?

In the original Greek, the term "glorify" here is pregnant with meaning. Jesus meant, "Magnify Me, celebrate Me, honor Me." It meant, "Adorn Me with luster," "Clothe Me with splendor," or "Impart glory to Me." When was the last time you knelt by your bed and said, "Father, make me famous so I can make you famous"?

The Word of God says you are made in His image. You should be like a magnifying glass through which people see Christ. To accomplish this Christ-like glow, He paid to make you shine. Pray, "Father, make me famous so I can make You famous."

This was God's original intention for the church.

What do you suppose stops people from doing this? I think it boils down to a misunderstanding of humility.

> *If my people who are called by my name humble themselves, and pray and seek my face and turn from their wicked ways, then I will hear from heaven and will forgive their sin and heal their land.* — ***1 Chronicles 7:14, NIV***

Scripture makes it clear that God desires His people to be humble. However, being humble does not mean doing nothing. Humility allows for God to do amazing things while giving the credit where it's due. That's what humility is.

It's About to Get Real…

I believe the last days are here, and it is of utmost importance that we as the church be what Jesus paid for: famous. Worldwide revival is not only near, it's necessary. I also believe that the world is set for one more pendulum swing. It is possible that God is about to re-ignite His church, because the promises that have to do with the latter days haven't come to pass yet.

The church must be visible, not hiding in the crevices. How else can we accomplish God's work?

God says, "Very truly I tell you, whoever believes in me will do the works I have been doing, and they will do even greater things than these" (John 14:12, NIV).

The Bible declares that the whole world will hear the gospel "and then the end will come" (Matthew 24:14, NIV). How is that going to happen?

The church must be visible, not hiding in the crevices. How else can we accomplish God's work? How will people believe in someone they've never heard of, and how will they hear unless *we* tell them?

In Acts 3, we see a perfect, temporal portrait of what Jesus taught as an eternal, church-wide reality. Peter and John had journeyed together to the temple at the hour of prayer, the ninth hour. Every day the same crippled man lay before the beautiful temple gate to beg for money from people as they entered. The man saw Peter and John approaching and asked them for help.

John and Peter responded, "Look at us!" Their first move was to put themselves in the limelight. The church in our community has to ask these questions. Why would that man know that Peter and John, who traveled daily to this place to pray, had something to offer? They had to have the "reputation" of meetings needs. Secondly, what would our community lack, if it lacked our church? If this answer is nothing … it's time to reorganize.

Their second move contains eternal significance. Peter says, "Silver or gold I do not have, but what I do have I give you. In the name of Jesus Christ of Nazareth, walk" (Acts 3:6, NIV). Take note that Peter was confident in what he had received. The authority he possessed was as real to him as the change in your pocket right now. When Jesus commissioned the church, His marching orders included this:

> *Heal the sick, cleanse the lepers, raise the dead, cast out demons. Freely you have received, freely give. — Matthew 10:8, NKJV*

You can't give what you don't have, and you can't receive something by faith that you don't believe. Peter was simply passing on what had been freely given to him. What was purchased for him was better than anything he could fabricate. What Christ bought is better than what we can build. We just have to know who in the heaven we are!

All of the people watching were amazed. When Peter saw the crowd's astonishment, he responded: "Men of Israel, why are you amazed at this, or why do you gaze at us, as if by our own power or piety we had made him walk? The God of Abraham, Isaac and Jacob, the God of our fathers, has glorified His servant Jesus" (Acts 3:12-13, NASB). This was a perfect picture of the church being the visible reflection of Jesus on this planet. "Look at us, now, look at Him." He would not have had the opportunity to lift up His savior without first stepping out in faith and believing he was exactly who Jesus paid for him to be.

Fame Leads to Multitudes

Jesus was walking by the Sea of Galilee when He saw two brothers, Simon (called Peter) and Andrew, Simon's brother, casting their nets into the sea. Jesus, knowing they were fishermen, said, "Follow me, and I will make you fishers of men" (Matthew 4:19, ESV). The Bible says they immediately left their nets and followed Him.

Notice Jesus did not say He would help them catch a lot of fish. He said, "*I will make you fishers of men.*" It was as if Jesus was telling these men that He was going to put them on the front lines and they would get their hands dirty. The New Testament does not say, "Believe and I will move mountains for you"; it says, "Believe and *you* will move mountains." A few verses later,

Scripture illustrates the fulfillment of what Jesus promised:

> *Jesus was going throughout all Galilee, teaching in their synagogues and proclaiming the gospel of the kingdom, and healing every kind of disease and every kind of sickness among the people. The news about Him spread throughout all Syria; and they brought to Him all who were ill, those suffering with various diseases and pains, demoniacs, epileptics, paralytics; and He healed them. —* ***Matthew 4:23-24, NASB***

After Jesus' fame spread, multitudes followed. Later, Acts 4 says, "But many of those who had heard the word believed, and the number of the men came to about five thousand."

After the apostles drew attention to themselves and then directed that attention to Jesus, five thousand people believed. This was revival! Their reckless display caused news to travel, and caused the hearts and eternities of 5,000 people to change that day.

What Is the Solution?

God took the children of Israel through a process that transformed them from being a lost, faithless and defeated group of complainers into being a faithful and sacrificial group of people who overcame.

Before coming into our faith, we are just as they are—broken, abandoned, abused, addicted. Jesus makes everyone who believes alive in Him. He forgives every trespass, and wipes out the law that stands against those who trust Him. He nailed every trespass to the cross. He disarmed every principality and power and made each a spectacle, triumphing over them for His children.

Every child of God received the identity needed to be famous, to overcome, to be wealthy, to be eternally rich, and to be made alive together with Christ.

This is my testimony, and it is the testimony of every believer. Those who believe in Jesus are made eternally alive. Nothing can establish dominion over the believer.

Joshua and the Israelites had a decision to make: to trust God, or to shrink back and allow their fear and disbelief dominate them. They chose to believe God and His promises to them. They went from circumcising all men one minute to marching into the most fortified city on the planet, at God's command. The Israelite army walked around the city six times. On the seventh day, they shouted as God commanded and the walls fell down.

Every child of God received the identity needed to be famous, to overcome, to be wealthy, to be eternally rich, and to be made alive together with Christ.

Let's return to Jericho. Just before the Israelites' mighty victory, Joshua approaches Jericho, looks up and sees a mysterious man standing before him. He asks, "Are you for us or are you against us?"

The man's reply is one of most profound statements in the whole Bible:

> *And he [the angel] said, 'No; but I am the commander of the army of the LORD. Now I have come.'* —***Joshua 1:5, ESV***

Are you for me, or against me? Seems like a straight question. No. Seems like a strange answer. But not in this case. This angel is telling Joshua that the mission was not about him. It's about God and His mission. The angel was not for or against anyone; He was directing Joshua to follow the Lord.

Remember Jesus's promise to make His disciples fishers of men? The disciples were in the same situation: Jesus was about His Father's business. They chose to follow the team that was guaranteed victory from before the foundation of the world, and indeed, thousands of people would eventually be saved because of their message.

It was not the children of Israel's obedience that knocked down the walls of Jericho. It was God. Joshua and his men decided to follow the commander of angel armies, and because they did, they gained the victory. This victory resulted in their fame spreading throughout the nation.

Do you think it was all that shouting on the seventh day that caused the army of Jericho to shut up the wall, so no one would come in or go out? No, it was God. He could have performed that miracle without the people's shouting. The point is, He wants to involve His people.

It's the same with the miracle of the loaves and fishes. Jesus fed 5,000 people from a few loaves and two fish. He could have just snapped His fingers and produced any amount of food needed. However, He wanted to involve the people in bringing Him glory. Jesus is always capable of taking what you have, and turning it into what He needs.

> *Jesus is always capable of taking what you have, and turning it into what He needs.*

The only path a child of God can take when choosing to follow Him is one of fruitfulness. God says, "This is to my Father's glory, that you bear much fruit, showing yourselves to be my disciples" (John 15:8, NIV). God is calling the church to be famous.

He desires people with undaunted obedience, the kind that drops their nets to follow Him. What keeps people from making that step is when they believe the lie that they don't have what it takes to be who God called them to be. They believe God's power is not great enough to accomplish what they are trying to accomplish. God's economy doesn't make sense. He can feed the world with only five loaves and two fish.

It's about faith. Step out and take the chance. Do what God's asking, and stop waiting for it to make sense.

Don't depend on self, or be discouraged because prayer didn't result in healing or someone's salvation. God's faithful. He'll take what is available, and turn it into something miraculous.

It is paramount that God's people come to the realization that the reproach of the past has been rolled away. They are no longer subject to their failures or limitations. In Christ, they have everything they need. The Creator of the universe makes His home in each person. *The fullness of God dwells in you.*

> *He kept all the laws, kept all the traditions, and only after he became the recipient of Gods grace did he write two-thirds of the New Testament and be named among the "ones who turned the world upside down."*

God gave you everything you need. Don't think for a second that he doesn't want to use you. Nobody's more "saved" than somebody else. The work He accomplished on the cross is sufficient *for you.* God is calling for this generation to be like Joshua, a generation that believes they are who God says they are.

In the book of Acts, there is a story about a man named Saul. Saul was a self-righteous, arrogant thug. He had permission to take anyone who followed Jesus captive. He oversaw the killing of some Christians and imprisonment of others. However, the Lord stopped Him on the road to Damascus and turned His world upside down.

At that moment, He gave his life to Jesus. God renamed him Paul instead of Saul, and within a short time he was proving that Jesus was the Christ. He was making Him famous within a few days. Paul was a recipient of the full gospel. This is the same grace available to everyone. What is also remarkable about Saul is that He dedicated his life to serving God in His own strength. He kept all of the laws and traditions, but only after he became the recipient of God's grace did he write two-thirds of the New Testament and be named among the "ones who turned the world upside down" (Acts 17:6, ESV). He thereby proved, yet again, that what He bought is far better than what we can build.

A believer in Jesus has already overcome and received it, at the moment of salvation. They simply need to walk in it.

Many believers have to continue to make themselves more righteous. But the human flesh will never be "more" righteous. There will never be that one and final provision to make a person's "old self" glorious. A believer in Jesus has already overcome and received it, at the moment of salvation. They simply need to walk in it.

CHAPTER THREE

Let's Give Them Something to Talk About

I thank my God through Jesus Christ for you all, that your faith is spoken of throughout the whole world. — **Romans 1:8, NIV**

God desires for His church to be famous in the world, but it's important to understand what God's heart is behind glorifying people to glorify Him. Since the dawn of the church, God's people have been inclined to doubt what God has for them. It's easier for people to say God loves them, and even easier to believe Jesus gave His life for the world. But it's really, really hard for people to personally believe Jesus *died as us, so that we could live as Him.* Consider the grammar of this passage:

Love has been perfected among us in this: that we may have boldness in the day of judgment; because as He is, so are we in this world. — ***1 John 4:17, NKJV***

The word "is" may seem simple, but it's important to dive into the tense in which it is used. Here the word is used in the present indicative tense, which means it is currently, actually happening. Therefore, as Jesus is right now—glorious, perfected, righteous, powerful, and eternal—so are we now!

At the beginning of Joshua 5, the Israelites were complaining about how many of their people had died in the wilderness. God had allowed many to perish because of their disobedience and lack of faith. They had built and worshipped idols. But by the end of Joshua 6:27, Scripture says God was with Joshua and his fame had spread throughout every nation.

> *What is the reputation of the church today? Does it "look like" Jesus?*

The church, from its foundation, was supposed to be a visible representation of Jesus in God's grand plan of redemption. What is the reputation of the church today? Does it "look like" Jesus? God's people certainly have the power and authority of Jesus. But is it visible? Do they perform more miracles than Jesus did?

In the past, I've thought this whole miracle-producing thing was a spiritual thing, something you would confess to make you feel better about what was before your very eyes. I knew His Word called me more than a conqueror through Christ who strengthens me. And for me, like most, this was merely a doctrinal reality and not and experiential reality. That was never God's intention, according to Scripture, and it certainly wasn't what Jesus modeled.

An entire generation of God's people was supposed to enter into a land promised to them by God, a land "flowing with milk and honey" (Exodus 33:3). But they ended up lost, wandering in the wilderness for almost forty years, and many died. To the Israelites, many likely questioned if God was a liar. Finally, someone decided they were going to agree with God. That the promise would finally come off the paper and into their lives to bear fruit that would not only change their generation, but the rest of the world.

It's common in the Christian world to say "amen" after praying. "Amen" is a very strong word, but not very many people know what it means. Simply put, it's agreeing with what is said. So, when the Lord says in Scripture that we are more than conquerors through Christ who strengthen us, saying "amen" means a person is in complete agreement with God. If we say we agree, then our lives should resemble what we are agreeing with.

Do we believe one church can see souls saved throughout the world? God designed the church to be famous.

If you are given the chance, find the closest unbelieving friend you have. Treat them to coffee and ask them some of the tough questions. What do they see when they look at you and your "church friends." Would they want what you have? Do they see what you confess as a solution or a problem?

Nine times out of ten, these questions don't need answered because we as Christian already know the answer. But that is not who I am called to be, and it's not who you are called to be. That first generation of people that were freed from bondage in Egypt saw God work miracles before their very eyes. They saw the Egyptian army defeated at the Red Sea. They saw God provide food for them daily while in the dessert. But when God made the BIG promise, total authority and total domination, they had a hard time believing Him.

He wasn't even asking for them to do much. Yes, they would need to fight, but God said *He* would drive them out! They live this sub-par life. However, God rose up a second generation of Israelites who trusted His promises. In a sense, they said "amen" to what God said.

The reputation of the early church was good; if anyone needed anything, the church provided it. People went to church before they went to a bank. It was so abundantly rich.

They believed they were going to a land flowing with milk and honey. Do we believe that? Do we believe one church can see souls saved throughout the world? God designed the church to be famous.

As a matter of fact, take out your Bible and read Galatians 1-2 and Colossians 2. The apostle Paul actually rebuked Peter for eating a wrong meal, stressing that eating a certain food doesn't make a person righteous. He reminded Peter what the grace of God had done in his life.

The Acts 2 church met in the temple daily. They studied and they prayed, and then they went house-to-house, breaking bread and fellowshipping with one another. They hung out; they relaxed.

They were glad and had simplicity of heart. This is the key. Scripture says they enjoyed "the favor of all the people. And the Lord added to their number daily those who were being saved" (Acts 2:47). The reputation of the early church was good; if anyone needed anything, the church provided it. People went to church before they went to a bank, it was so abundantly rich.

If people needed healing, the church was so abundantly powerful, people went to the church before they would go to the hospital. The church gave with great gladness, healed, and prayed. It was like a mirror for the world to see Jesus.

If your church is anything like mine, you have an "inviting culture"; if you don't yet, you should. I see new people come in our doors, and we get incredible feedback. Allow me to show you something in Scripture that will revolutionize your vision, your expectation, and the way you see yourself as a reflection of the King you serve:

> *Now when the queen of Sheba heard of the fame of Solomon concerning the name of the LORD, she came to test him with hard questions. She came to Jerusalem with a very great retinue, with camels that bore spices, very much gold, and precious stones; and when she came to Solomon, she spoke with him about all that was in her heart. So Solomon answered all her questions; there was nothing so difficult for the king that he could not explain it to her. And when the queen of Sheba had seen all the wisdom of Solomon, the house that he had built, the food on his table, the seating of his servants, the service of his waiters and their apparel, his cupbearers, and his entryway by which he went up to the house of the LORD, there was no more spirit in her. Then she said to the king: "It was a true report which I heard in my own land about your words and your wisdom. However I did not believe the words until I came and saw with my own eyes; and indeed the half was not told me. Your wisdom and prosperity exceed the fame of which I heard. Happy are your men and happy are these your servants, who stand continually before you and hear your wisdom! Blessed be the LORD your God, who delighted in you, setting you on the throne of Israel! Because the LORD has loved Israel forever, therefore He made you king, to do justice and righteousness."* — ***1 Kings 10:1-9, NKJV***

Let's revisit the queen's response to what she visibly saw with her own two eyes: "Your wisdom and prosperity exceed the *fame* of which I heard. Happy are your men and happy are these your servants, who stand continually before you and hear your wisdom! Blessed be the *LORD* your God." She admitted that she did not *believe* until she *saw*. Whose fame did she perceive? It was King Solomon's. Who got the credit? "Blessed be the *LORD* your God."

The more often people see us, the church, reflecting what our Savior already paid for, the more they see Him. We cannot, and should not, shy away from excellence in order to appease religious people. It is paramount that we be on display. My Bible says this:

> *You are the light of the world. A city that is set on a hill cannot be hidden. Nor do they light a lamp and put it under a basket, but on a lampstand, and it gives light to all who are in the house. Let your light so shine before men, that they may see your good works and glorify your Father in heaven.* — ***Matthew 5:14-16, NKJV***

Whose good works? Who gets the glory?

We want to give people who are watching something to talk about. Christians already have a reputation. Let's give them something tremendous to talk about!

The Bible says the Son of Man did not come into this world to condemn the world, so why would His church? The church isn't here for that reason anyway.

> *I thank my God through Jesus Christ for you all, that your faith is spoken of throughout the whole world.* — ***Romans 1:8, NIV***

Paul wrote to the Romans how thankful he was for their faith, acknowledging that the whole known world at the time knew about it. These Christians obviously were causing a stir, and clearly others were talking about what they were seeing.

> *The more people see us, the church, reflecting what our Savior already paid for, the more they see Him*

Why would somebody talk about *you*? What do people say about the church? It may not always be positive, but remember: Jesus said, *If the world hates you, keep in mind that it hated me first* (John 15:18, paraphrased). He warned that Christians would be reviled, hated, tortured, and persecuted for His name's sake.

How can Christians balance this, knowing that following Jesus will result in persecution, but also that Christians should have favor with all people? We see in the Gospels that not everyone hated Jesus' church. It was a specific group of people the Bible refers to as Pharisees. Religious people hated the church because it represented a system that was counterintuitive to their doctrine of justification by works; therefore, they believed, it had to be evil. The sinners, however, loved the church. In the book of Acts, we see that the community was ready to kill the Pharisees for threatening to take the apostles (Acts 5:26).

When Christians love as Jesus did, people will love them. Paul wrote in Romans 5:8 that while people were yet sinners, Christ died for them. This is our example of love for the world. I once heard a pastor offer this question as a form of self-diagnosis: What does this community lose, if it loses you?

The Bible does not say, "For the world so loved God that He gave His only son." It wasn't a mutual transaction. He was motivated to give by His love for humanity, and nothing else. That's how to become famous. That's how Christians are held in a positive light.

This is what it means to be a "city on a hill" or "salt of the earth." It means to keep the light of Jesus burning. Don't make Him look bad, but beautiful. And He will accomplish what He needs to accomplish.

> *Jesus lifted His eyes to heaven and He said, Father the hour is come glorify your Son, so that your Son may glorify you.* —***John 17:1, NIV***

Put me in the limelight so I can point everyone toward you, Father. That should be the Christian's prayer. Jesus Himself prayed it. When He prayed, He said, "I pray this prayer for the people around me because I know who you are, but I want them to know that it's you that's glorifying me." Isn't that amazing?

CHAPTER FOUR

Jesus Face-palmed

Jesus also offered a soft rebuke in John 11 regarding not only what our faith should be placed in, but *when*. Disbelief is often what prevents most people from walking in the fame that Jesus calls them to. People don't believe God will come through, so they try to control their life on their own.

Mary, Martha, and Lazarus were dear friends of Jesus, but Lazarus became sick. His sisters came to inform Jesus, who waited two days before going to see him. By that time, Lazarus had died. And by the time He arrived, Lazarus had been dead four days, and the Bible says … he stunk.

Jesus tells Martha that her brother will rise again. Martha responds, "I know that he will rise again in the resurrection on the last day." When I imagine Jesus and Mary walking along the way, and she thinks that Jesus plans to fix this problem in eternity and not now, I see Jesus break stride—and face-palm. As if He looked at Mary and said, "Who do you think you're talking to?"

As with all of His promises concerning you, me, and the church, Jesus was not talking about later. He was talking about now! Jesus proceeded to bring Lazarus back to life, after which He said, "Did I not tell you that if you believe, you will see the glory of God?" (John 11:40, NIV).

We need to quit trying to rationalize, and take God at His Word.

This simple rebuke reminded Martha of whom Jesus was. Jesus then asked His Father to bring Lazarus back to life, "for the benefit of the people standing here, that they may believe that you sent me" (John 11:42, NIV). Jesus brought attention to Himself for the purpose of bringing glory to God.

As Christians, we have to agree with Jesus. In this case, Jesus said, "He is going to rise." He never said "on the last day." Like Martha, Christians sometimes try to make sense of things in the Bible that don't make sense. We need to quit trying to rationalize, and take God at His Word. When we start weighing odds, we inevitably begin to doubt Him. The gentle rebuke He offered Martha in modern English would probably be something like, "Martha! Did I say later? I said now!" After all, Hebrews 11—the Book of Faith, as some scholars refer to it—does not say, "Later, faith is…"; rather, it says, "*Now* faith is…"

Jesus walked up to Lazarus's grave and commanded the stone to roll away, and Lazarus miraculously walked out. Jesus wants to be glorified now, not later! The calling is to be like Jesus *now*. Jesus was famous; people came from everywhere to hear His teachings. Multitudes followed Him because of who He was.

Jesus, who knew no sin, became sin so that the people He loves would become the righteousness of God. This righteousness is for *now*, not later.

> *I am the resurrection and the life. Whoever believes in me, though he die, yet shall he live. Whoever lives and believes in me will never die. —* ***John 11:25, ESV***

Then Jesus asked the famous question: "Do you believe this?" Mary responded, "Yes, Lord; I believe that you are the Christ, the Son of God, who is coming into the world" (John 11:26-27, ESV).

What does the Bible say about Christians? That they are the righteousness of God. The Word says Jesus has been given authority over every principality, power, might, and dominion and that He then gave that authority to Christians (Ephesians 1:21-23). God delegated.

One of my favorite writings about this is found in Paul's Letter to the Colossians. It starts with a warning:

> *Beware lest anyone cheat you through philosophy and empty deceit, according to the tradition of men, according to the basic principles of the world, and not according to Christ. —* ***Colossians 2:8, NKJV***

Paul was making sure this church knew that what Jesus had paid for didn't fit in their system of their thinking.

> *For in Him dwells all the fullness of the Godhead bodily; and you are complete in Him, who is the head of all principality and power.* — **Colossians 2:9-10, NKJV**

We have to do a small Greek lesson here to capture fully what Paul is trying to communicate. The Greek word for "fullness" and the Greek word for "complete" are the same Greek word used in different tenses. Here are the definitions, respectively:

"Fullness" (*plērōma*) describes that which is (has been) filled.

"Complete" (*plēroō*) is to make full, to fill up, to cause to abound, to furnish or supply liberally.

If Paul's message could be restated using the definitions in place of the translated words, it would describe our transcendent relationship with God this way: "All of God lives in Jesus, and all of Jesus lives in us." It doesn't make sense that we could be co-equal with Christ, but the Bible says exactly that.

The Radical and Powerful Grace of God

What is the church doing with that resurrection power? The apostle Paul was very clear what he expected the church to be doing! Paul wrote many encouraging letters to churches filled with people who weren't walking in the promises of God. Some letters began by correcting the envy, strife, and division among those in the church. He shared the gospel in his letters. *Paul gave people something to talk about.*

However, Paul wasn't always living his life in a manner pleasing to God. It wasn't until he had a dramatic encounter with the risen Christ that his life changed.

In Acts 9, Jesus has already died and ascended. The New Testament church was in its formative stages, preaching the gospel of Jesus. But Saul, a Pharisee at the highest level, persecuted and killed Christians. This man (who later refers to himself as the chief of sinners) met Jesus in an extraordinary way on the road to Damascus. Saul fell to the ground in the presence of the Lord.

Well aware of Saul's attempts to kill Christians, Jesus asked Saul why he was persecuting *Him*. Paul asked, "Who are you, Lord?"

"I am Jesus, whom you are persecuting," Jesus replied. (Acts 9:5, NIV)

The grace of God was radical and powerful, temporarily blinding Paul. Meanwhile God was having a conversation with a man name Ananias, instructing him to go find Paul. Ananias was resistant, knowing full well this man killed Christians. But God had a purpose for Paul and an assignment for Ananias: to baptize the man who would impact the growth of the early church more than any other.

> *So Ananias departed and entered the house, and after laying his hands on him said, 'Brother Saul, the Lord Jesus, who appeared to you on the road by which you were coming, has sent me so that you may regain your sight and be filled with the Holy Spirit.'* —***Acts 9:17, NASB***

Immediately something like scales fell from Paul's eyes. His eyesight returned, he arose, and he was baptized. He received food and was strengthened.

In recounting this miracle in the life of Paul, there are phrases and words that bear notice: *immediately, at once, a few days.* In one day, Paul went from being a man that killed Christians to a man filled with the Spirit of God, who started the first-century church on his own. He didn't sit and think about it for a few months, or walk around the mountain for forty days, sad and sorry for what he had done. He didn't have to pay that price anymore, because he had met Jesus. Jesus immediately and radically changed Paul. The reproach of his past was gone; he was a new man, a new creation in Christ.

Acts 9 reports that Paul went around to the towns, proclaiming that Jesus was the Christ. Here is another example of someone making Jesus famous through his life. That's the promise that you and I have been given, too. In Christ, believers are able, by His power, to make Him famous.

Paul wasn't just any Jew. He was the chief Jew, a rabbi above rabbis. He had memorized the first five books of the Bible, the Torah, and was an expert at following the law. After believing in Jesus, he began to understand God's grace.

> *For I would have you know, brethren, that the gospel which was preached by me is not according to man. For I neither received it from man, nor was I taught it, but I received it through a revelation of Jesus Christ. For you have heard of my former manner of life in Judaism, how I used to persecute the church of God beyond measure and tried to destroy it; and I was advancing in Judaism beyond many of my contemporaries among my countrymen, being more extremely zealous for my ancestral traditions. But when God, who had set me apart even from my mother's womb and called me through His grace, was pleased. —* **Galatians 1:11-15, NASB**

Paul made it clear that the gospel he received did not come from any human being, but from the revelation of Jesus Christ alone.

This conversation Paul was having with the Galatians was the same kind you and I can have with people every day. Experiencing Jesus' unconditional love and favor transformed Paul into something the law could never achieve: His own image. Paul went from killing Christians to proving that Jesus was the Christ. He reminded the Galatians of his former conduct in Judaism, how he persecuted the church of God and tried to destroy it, and how he put the traditions of his fathers as the highest goal in his life.

> *Imagine finding out that your testimony was so renowned that it had spread throughout the state you lived in by word of mouth?*

Paul writes how he was traveling around, preaching the gospel, and arrived at a church where nobody knew him by sight:

"Then I went into the regions of Syria and Cilicia. I was still unknown by sight to the churches of Judea which were in Christ; but only, they kept hearing, 'He who once persecuted us is now preaching the faith which he once tried to destroy.' And they were glorifying God because of me" (Galatians 1:21-24).

People had never seen Paul, but they had heard of him as the one who used to persecute Christians, but was now preaching Christ. Because of Paul's radical testimony and transformation, 1 Galatians 11:24 says, "they were glorifying God because of me." Can you imagine Paul's reaction?

Imagine finding out that your testimony was so renowned that it had spread by word of mouth throughout the state you lived in?

Paul gave the Galatians something to talk about.

Prior to his transformation, Paul was not unlike many people sitting in the pews today. Scripture says he was "exceedingly zealous for the traditions of his fathers." How many people in church today follow man's traditions, the "things we have always done," before God's instruction in the Word of God?

Be the Visible Representation of Jesus

When Lazarus's sister came to Jesus, grieving over her brother's death, He comforted her with the truth that Lazarus would be resurrected *now*, not sometime in the future. You too are not a work-in-progress. Rather, you're a work completed 2,000 years ago at the cross of Christ.

Joshua and his men were so zealous, they cut off their foreskins with flint knives to be who God called them to be. They had tenacity to pursue righteousness. Scripture commands us to pursue righteousness—to go after it zealously and to run the race with perseverance. Yet we must realize that righteousness was a gift, not a reward.

We are not to expect our problems to be solved in eternity. Demand heaven now. Demand what Jesus paid for now! This is how the world will be saved.

Passionately pursue righteousness, and turn from the past. He has changed you inside and out. Your life is what Jesus paid for on the cross. Jesus paid for your life. Make every effort to give Jesus what is rightly His!

Pursue righteousness, faith, love, and peace with others who call on the Lord out of a pure heart.

When Paul was approaching death, he poured his heart out to his young friend, Timothy, who had stayed by Paul's side in ministry. He encouraged Timothy to "flee from youthful lusts and pursue righteousness, faith, love and peace, with those who call on the Lord from a pure heart" (2 Timothy 2:22, NASB).

What does this mean for us? Don't look back. The reproach of Egypt is gone. Pursue righteousness, faith, love, and peace with others who call on the Lord out of a pure heart. The original Greek word for "flee" literally means "to pursue, run swiftly, or catch."

Toward the end of 2 Timothy, Paul writes that he fought the good fight. It wasn't some passive "hallelujah!" He ran the race of life to completion. He finished strong.

Follow Paul's example. Don't settle for less than the promise of God. There are few things God *can't* do, and one of them is lie!

Stand on God's promises, and be in agreement with them. Doing this will align yourself with God. This is what the prophet Amos meant when he said, "Do two walk together unless they have agreed to do so?" (Amos 3:3, NIV). When a person "walks together" with God, nothing can stop them! God will drive enemies out from before them, and they will "take the land."

God wants you visible. He wants you famous. This is Christianity. It has nothing to do with you, but about God's name and reputation. Be a picture of love to the unlovable, a picture of generosity to those in need.

Jesus' last words at the end of the book of Matthew were to go preach the gospel to all nations, making disciples and baptizing them in the name of the Father, the Son, and the Holy Spirit.

Agree with this promise!

God wants you visible. He wants you famous. This is Christianity. It has nothing to do with you, but it is about God's name and reputation. Be a picture of love to the unlovable, a picture of generosity to those in need. Be selfless, and be the salt of the earth. This is the gospel, and it is powerful.

When you do what no one else will do, when you go where no one else will go, when you give when no one else will give, that's when you become famous.

When you sacrifice what no one else will sacrifice, people see Jesus, and that's who God designed you to be. You are God's workmanship and His masterpiece. You were not created to hide under a basket! You were meant to be high on a hill for everybody to see.

CHAPTER FIVE

God Delegated

Blessed are the meek: for they shall inherit the earth. "And He put all things under His feet, and gave Him to be head over all things to the church, which is His body, the fullness of Him who fills all in all. — ***Ephesians 1:22-23, NASB***

God designed the church to be known throughout all the nations of the world. In the early years of the church, the faith of new believers was tremendous. It was so spectacular that it got people talking. They were imitating Jesus, the model for all believers.

Jesus was willing to be made a spectacle for the sake of God's name. We have to ask ourselves if we are willing to do the same.

Greater Works Than These

Very truly I tell you, whoever believes in me will do the works I have been doing, and they will do even greater things than these, because I am going to the Father. — ***John 14:12, NIV***

Jesus told His disciples they would perform greater works than the works He did. The psalmist echoed Jesus's prayer, writing: "May you increase my greatness and turn to comfort me" (Psalms 71:21, NASB). How many people can say they prayed like that last night?

For some reason, many people take on false humility. This does nothing but hinder the gospel from going out. And if the gospel is not preached, people will perish. Nobody will "see" Jesus. God did not intend for Christians to keep silent or hide.

In the early years of Jesus' ministry, people came from around the country to hear Him teach. He was famous, but the miraculous thing is, He imparted that magnificent glory to each and every believer. God delegated the responsibility of making Himself known to others. Take a close look at Jesus pray in John 17:

> *I do not pray for these alone, but also for those who will believe in Me through their word; that they all may be one, as You, Father, are in Me, and I in You; that they also may be one in Us, that the world may believe that You sent Me. And the glory which You gave Me I have given them, that they may be one just as We are one: I in them, and You in Me; that they may be made perfect in one, and that the world may know that You have sent Me, and have loved them as You have loved Me.* — ***John 17:20-23, NKJV***

There are a few things here we need to dig into a little more deeply. Jesus prayed to the Father and said that He had given us the glory the Father had given Him.

The word "given" here bears more depth than meets the eye. This word in the Greek specifically meant that something was *undeservedly* given, or unearned. Accordingly, it is important that we realize the promises of Jesus are received by grace through faith, *not* by our works. If we miss this truth, we will never believe that the promise is ours for the taking.

Furthermore, the glory (*doxa*) we were given is this, according to the Strong's Concordance: "the kingly majesty which belongs to him as supreme ruler, majesty in the sense of the absolute perfection of the deity."

Read that again, and realize that Jesus undeservedly gave God's opinion of Him *to you*. Tell me again how the church cannot be visible, famous, and victorious?

The books of Exodus and Joshua recount the story of the Israelites, stuck in bondage in Egypt. This was a shadow of the reality of Christians today who are also stuck in bondage or sin. They are stuck in the world.

God did something supernatural when He led Israel out of Egypt into a place called the "wilderness." It was here in this desolate place that God developed them into a people He could use, who would inherit the promise.

Notice the progression: they were delivered from Egypt, baptized in the Red Sea, and then led into the wilderness. This was part of God's process to make them holy and righteous, a people He could use.

God knew what was ahead for Israel when they arrived at the Promised Land. They would see war and be attacked by other evil nations. Had God not prepared them, they may have turned back in fear. So, He took them through this refining process and instilled the desire of heaven in their hearts.

As soon as Israel was set apart and in the land, God began to delegate. Israel was to begin tilling ground, planting seed, and bearing fruit.

For forty years, bread literally rained down from heaven. The Israelites didn't have to do anything for themselves. It was as if God coddled them the whole way. Once Israel was ready to bear fruit, the bread stopped. Now, God was going to give Israel some responsibility to provide and bear fruit in the land. God delivered them, and God developed them. The reproach of their past was gone, and they were ready.

The first thing God required of them in the new land was circumcision. This act was highly symbolic for a rolling away of their past. Their years of unbelief were behind them; they were moving forward, committed to God's purposes for them.

As soon as Israel was set apart and in the land, God began to delegate. Israel was to begin tilling ground, planting seed, and bearing fruit.

Israel would begin to accomplish things on God's behalf. The whole time they were journeying through the wilderness, the people's garments and sandals never wore out. Once they entered the Promised Land, they started falling apart. Why? Now that His people had been delivered and developed, it was now time to delegate.

If the worship team crashes and burns during a church service, is the senior leader responsible? Not at all. That leader delegated authority to make that worship experience as he saw fit. The senior leader's responsibility is removed. Just as the book of Ephesians says that God gave the church power over all things, that worship leader was given all power and authority.

Why Is It So Important to Understand That God Delegated?

I had a conversation with a young lady the other day. She was wrestling with why God let something terrible happen in her life. I tried to explain to her this concept of God delegating responsibility, and the negative effects that sometimes result. I tried to explain to her about His purposes in delegating.

God sends His people as delegates on His behalf. Believers are called *ambassadors*. 2 Corinthians 5:20 says: "We are therefore Christ's ambassadors, as though God were making his appeal through us. We implore you on Christ's behalf: Be reconciled to God" (NIV).

When an ambassador travels to another country, they represent, say, the United States. These ambassadors act on the president's behalf. They possess the credentials of high-ranking officials of their home government, and they maintain such rights as an ambassador. When they are sent to another country, they aren't sent with the authority of a janitor; they are legally given the authority of the king or president of their homeland to act in that country.

> *There is nothing above Jesus. There is none greater; He is the beginning and the end, the Alpha, the Omega. He's the King of kings, the Lord of lords and the Prince of peace.*

This is what God calls us to be! We are His representation in the world. We are citizens of heaven sent to the citizens of the earth. Just as Jesus represented God while He was on earth, we are Jesus's physical representation on earth. It's profound! We are responsible for being as famous as He was because of the mighty works that He does through us.

God took His hands off us and gave us responsibility and all authority to change the world. Remember, God promised to extol wisdom and revelation to those who love Him, and to open their eyes to understand the power of His greatness towards the saints.

The same power that raised Jesus from the dead works in us. Scripture says God put all things under Jesus' feet. He had control over death, sickness, disease, and the devil and his demons. He stepped on each one of their heads as He climbed to His position at the right hand of the Father.

There is nothing above Jesus. There is none greater; He is the beginning and the end, the Alpha, the Omega. He's the King of kings, the Lord of lords, and the Prince of peace. He possesses all things, and He had power in His very words to spin Earth into existence. He then gave over all these things *to the church*, which is His representation on earth, the fullness of Him. God has delegated the responsibility of changing this world to *you*.

Do you believe it?

> *We have to believe that the gospel is true, and that we have power and authority over all things.*

I look at so many little faces that haven't experienced evil yet, that know nothing but innocence, and I'm reminded of the people responsible with changing the world—and I have to hold back tears. It's our job as the church to represent Jesus to them. We have to believe that the gospel is true and that we have power and authority over all things.

We have to be the church that God has intended for us to be. We cannot miss this calling and mask it with a false humility that says we are not good enough. False humility is not humility at all. It is the epitome of arrogance. False humility is thinking you are better than someone else for thinking so little of your self. How much more hypocritical could we be, not to mention counterproductive!

You and I have the mind of Christ (1 Corinthians 2:16). This is not an opinion; it is the Word of God. God says He has removed your heart of stone and replaced it with a heart of flesh.

What's the difference between you and me, and the children of Israel? There is no difference. God delivers, develops, and then delegates. All He asks of us is to believe.

Why Do We Forfeit Our Fame?

There are three biblical reasons why Christians forfeit their fame, and interestingly, they can be found in the story of the nation of Israel: failure, focus, and fear.

1. **Failure**

After the children of Israel fled Egypt, they were a mess. If they even had the chance to enter the Promise Land in that condition, God would have turned them back. They needed a lot of cleaning up!

Jesus was crucified, buried, and then raised from the dead. We can identify with all three parts of that sacrifice. When Jesus died on the cross, so did our sinful nature, and so did the law that opposed us. When Jesus was buried, our sinful nature was buried with Him. And

His resurrection gave Him all authority—this is where we gain our authority, too. That's the gospel.

Believing this acquits us of sin; we now exhibit the righteousness of God in Christ Jesus. Our identity is no longer earned; it's assigned and it's perfect. If you believe the gospel, then you're a new creation.

For Christians, our ability is based on nothing but His accomplishments. Remember, Israel finally reached the place where the reproach of their past was rolled away. Jesus rolled it away 2,000 years ago for us too: on the cross.

Why does the fear of failure still haunt Christians and keep them from claiming the fame God desires for them? Fear of failure leads to forfeiture of our position in Christ.

It is a fear of past failures, by which saved people believe their current ability is dependent on past accomplishments; but this is a lie, and opposite of what the Word of God teaches. For Christians, our ability is based on nothing but His accomplishments. Remember, Israel finally reached the place where the reproach of their past was rolled away. Jesus rolled it away 2,000 years ago for us too: on the cross.

Many people live in a place of defeat because they doubt this truth and, therefore, don't inherit the promise. They believe these lies:

- I can't go out and preach to people because I'm not that smart.
- I can't be around crowds of people because I have social anxiety.
- I can't minister to the poor or the needy because I don't have enough money.

This is not who the Christian is! Followers of Jesus are given new assignments and the power and authority to complete them. They *are* the love of Christ. They are anointed and called for specific, unique purposes, solely to manifest the Son of God to the world.

For this reason, God has healed our bodies and destroyed the works of the wicked one. We are all recipients of this undeserved grace. If God has called you to something that seems beyond what you are able to do on your own, then you are in the right position with God. If it weren't beyond your capability, you wouldn't need Him to accomplish it.

> *But God chose the foolish things of the world to shame the wise; God chose the weak things of the world to shame the strong.* — **1 Corinthians 1:27, NIV**

God used a young shepherd boy to defeat a giant. The odds don't matter to God, and when Christians start weighing them, they start doubting Him.

Moses believed God throughout the time he lead the Israelites in the desert. Sadly, when it was time to cross over into the Promised Land, that belief waivered:

> *Then the Lord spoke to Moses saying, "Send out for yourself men so that they may spy out the land of Canaan, which I am going to give to the sons of Israel; you shall send a man from each of their fathers' tribes, every one a leader among them."h—* ***Numbers 13:1-2, NASB***

God had promised Israel that they would wipe out their enemies, plunder everything they had, and continue on to possess the land.

Moses and the Israelites were just about to enter the land of Canaan. It was just beyond their reach! Moses instructed men to spy out the land, the first sign of trouble. God had already given the nation of Israel the land back in Genesis 12:7, promising it to them as an inheritance. Nonetheless, Moses sent the spies on mission, hoping for a good report.

God had promised Israel that they would wipe out their enemies, plunder everything they had, and continue on to possess the land. Most importantly, God promised He would be with them for the whole journey.

The spies returned to give their report. Numbers 13:30 recounts that Caleb quieted the people before Moses and said, "We should by all means go up and take possession of it, for we will surely overcome it" (Numbers 13:30, NIV). He was confident in God's promises. Though the people were as giants, Caleb knew who Israel's strength was.

However, the other men who had been sent out with Caleb to spy came back with a different report: "We are not able to go up against the people, for they are too strong for us" (Numbers 13:31, NIV). They complained the people were bigger and stronger, and numerous "like grasshoppers" in their eyes. If they entered the land, they would be devoured.

If you think you are sinful and weak and aren't equipped for the job, the enemy will see you this way too.

One of the reasons that we forfeit our fame is our fear of failure, but failure is not a reality in the Kingdom of God. God had promised Israel the land, and He would be faithful to His Word; the men of Israel doubted their own ability to defeat the enemy nations. Though they had seen God's kindness and faithfulness, they couldn't see past their own fear.

If you think you are sinful and weak and aren't equipped for the job, the enemy will see you this way, too. But this is not what God says. Take a close look at what the spy reports in Numbers:

> *There we saw the giants (the descendants of Anak came from the giants); and we were like grasshoppers* in our own sight, *and so we were in their sight." —* ***Numbers 13:33, NKJV***

Their perception of themselves was skewed, they saw themselves as weak and small, and as the Word says, "As a man thinks, so he is." The giants' perception of the army of Israel was given to them by the army themselves. We've used this "test," if you will, in our leadership circles. Try it with yourself:

I was like __________ in my own sight, so I am __________ in theirs.

Who you believe you are makes all the difference.

Inherit the promises of God, and go without hindrance. If you let your past experiences continue to dictate your future movement in the Kingdom of God, then you will stay right where you are until the day you leave this earth.

2. **Focus**

> *For whoever wishes to save his life will lose it; but whoever loses his life for My sake will find it. —* ***Matthew 16:25, NASB***

Those who become tenaciously focused on Jesus and are able to cast aside their own cares will gain much. However, some people let the cares of the world dictate everything they do. Some people receive the Word of God with gladness but then let it slip away, choked out by the cares of this life. They can't focus on Jesus and the assignment at hand, and thus forfeit their fame.

Satan is a master at making people think 1) their circumstances are worse than they seem, or 2) they will never be able to fix the situation.

Some don't truly believe seeking God's Kingdom first will result in better things being added to their life. Satan plays on this, and one of the key ways in this generation is to make followers of Jesus so busy and distracted, they lose focus on their family, their ministry, their calling, and on Jesus. The result? They forfeit their fame.

Satan is a master at making people think 1) their circumstances are worse than they seem, or 2) they will never be able to fix the situation.

This is why Jesus exhorted His disciples to "watch and pray always," in regard to the rapture of the church so that the cares of this world would not weigh them down. Jesus gives this same encouragement to us. Satan attempts to steal away God's promises using this tactic.

In Joshua 7, a man named Achan forfeited the promise from God because of a loss of focus. Israel had just circumcised their male population, conquered Jericho, and crossed the Jordan. The enemy nations were terrified of Israel! Scripture says the nations "melted in fear" of the Israelites (Joshua 2:11). These nations knew the Lord was with them, and they were terrified. Israel's fame had spread throughout the entire world.

The children of Israel fled like sissies from this tiny enemy army, even though God had previously told them no nation would be able to stand against them.

Then, a chapter later, one man loses focus: Achan. This time Israel sent spies out into the country. They returned with a plan to send a few thousand men to wipe out the enemy. "We'll be fine," they said! Instead, thirty-six Israelites were killed before the battle began. The children of Israel fled like sissies from this tiny enemy army, even though God had previously told them no nation would be able to stand against them. But that promise was conditional on their focus—on their meditation of the Word, on their understanding of the Law, and on their focus on the promise at hand.

Joshua was on his face before God. In Joshua 7:10, the Lord commanded Joshua to get up off his face. Then

God informed Joshua of why the Israelites were defeated: someone within Israel had transgressed God's covenant. They stole some items God had commanded be set apart for Him alone, and worse yet, hid those things among their own belongings.

Israel, called to a land "flowing with milk and honey," fell apart. One man, Achan, was afraid he would go without. He didn't believe the promise of God was true. He didn't believe God would take care of him. So he took care of himself and stole the devoted things. Achan lost focus of the task at hand and literally forfeited fame by losing his life.

> *Why have you brought this trouble on us? The LORD will bring trouble on you today." Then all Israel stoned him, and after they had stoned the rest, they burned them.* —***Joshua 7:25, NIV***

God reminded the children of Israel—as well as Achan and his entire family—that He had delegated a serious responsibility to the people of Israel. It was paramount that they follow His instructions. Israel broke the covenant, not God! Israel needed to focus on the task at hand, not the pursuit of this life.

3. **Fear**

In the book of Isaiah, the prophet received a revelation from the Lord. Isaiah had come to a place where he finally saw God for who He is in all His glory.

Immediately, he declares, "I am a man of unclean lips!" (Isaiah 6:5, NIV).

Next Isaiah says, "And I live among a people of unclean lips, and my eyes have seen the King, the Lord Almighty" (Isaiah 6:5, NIV).

God supernaturally put coal on Isaiah's lips, and transformed him into a new man. And He did the same for us: He supernaturally cleansed you and me.

Immediately God revealed to Isaiah a vision of who Isaiah was in the present, versus who Isaiah was in the past. Isaiah knew God was in relationship with him, and he knew what his task at hand was. He was a prophet to the nations. He was to go set things in the right order according to the Word of God.

God supernaturally put coal on Isaiah's lips and transformed him into a new man. And He did the same for us: He supernaturally cleansed you and me.

Jesus told a parable in Matthew 25:14-25 that paints a picture of what happens when a follower of Jesus loses focus:

"Again, it will be like a man going on a journey, who called his servants and entrusted his wealth to them. To one he gave five bags of gold, to another two bags, and to another one bag, each according to his ability. Then he went on his journey. The man who had received five bags of gold went at once and put his money to work and gained five bags more. So also, the one with two bags of gold gained two more. But the man who had received one bag went off, dug a hole in the ground and hid his master's money.

"You have been faithful with a few things; I will put you in charge of many things. Come and share your master's happiness!"(Matt. 25:23)

"After a long time the master of those servants returned and settled accounts with them. The man who had received five bags of gold brought the other five. 'Master,' he said, 'you entrusted me with five bags of gold. See, I have gained five more.' His master replied, 'Well done, good and faithful servant! You have been faithful with a few things; I will put you in charge of many things. Come and share your master's happiness!'

"The man with two bags of gold also came. 'Master,' he said, 'you entrusted me with two bags of gold; see, I have gained two more.' His master replied, 'Well done, good and faithful servant! You have been faithful with a few things; I will put you in charge of many things. Come and share your master's happiness!'

"Then the man who had received one bag of gold came. 'Master,' he said, 'I knew that you are a hard man, harvesting where you have not sown and gathering where you have not scattered seed. So I was afraid and went out and hid your gold in the ground. See, here is what belongs to you.'" (Matthew 25:14-25, NIV)

> *But the third servant did not receive such high praise. What was this servant afraid of? He wasn't afraid of failure. He wasn't afraid of criticism. He was afraid of God.*

In this parable, Jesus described heaven as being like a man who had traveled to a far country but then called his servants to evaluate what each had done with what they were given. The first two servants were praised for investing well. Their master, God, acknowledged their faithfulness over a few things and promised to make them rulers over many things.

But the third servant did not receive such high praise. What was this servant afraid of? He wasn't afraid of failure. He wasn't afraid of criticism. *He was afraid of God.* It was as if the third servant was saying, "I know that you are the Creator of the universe and that you're all-powerful. I know you make something out of nothing, and I was scared to death of you. So I hid what you gave me in the ground." Unfortunately, this was not an accurate understanding of the character of God. The third servant's information about the master was right; the master himself didn't deny it. However, his information about himself and his standing with the master was wrong.

> *How can the church fail, when it is His hands and feet walking on the planet? The church is a new creation!*

God doesn't oppose those who believe; in fact, He gives His children something to care for. He gives them His authority, His power, and everything else needed to be famous.

He who is with you will be in you. The same power that was with Moses was with Joshua and now dwells in His people, the church. How can the church fail when it is His hands and feet, walking on the planet? The church is a new creation!

> *Therefore, if anyone is in Christ, the new creation has come: The old has gone, the new is here! —* ***2 Corinthians 5:17, NIV***

God reconciled sinful man to Himself through Jesus Christ. He's given us the ministry of reconciliation, and He has made us ambassadors.

> *Therefore, we are ambassadors for Christ, as though God were making an appeal through us; we beg you on behalf of Christ, be reconciled to God. He made Him who knew no sin to be sin on our behalf, so that we might become the righteousness of God in Him. —* ***2 Corinthians 5:20, NASB***

We don't have to be delivered into a place of failure to be delivered into a place of prosperity and fruitfulness. Paul encouraged these people to stop settling for mediocrity, and stop depending on past failures. In Christ, all things have been made new. In order to be the people God called us to be, we have to have a right understanding of who we are in Christ.

We also have to have a right understanding of the circumstances that we have been placed in and the ministry we have been called to. Most importantly, we have to have a proper understanding of our relationship with God. God is not far away, or waiting to condemn, like the third servant believed. He is near, and ready to help His people.

As an ambassador of Christ, know that God approves of you and has commissioned you. That's all that matters. That's where fame comes from.

God wants to reveal Himself to you in your circumstances. You don't have to leave that circumstance to come find Him! He'll find you there. Whether it's a difficult marriage or a frightening health situation, God wants to reveal Himself to you right where you are.

Surrender to the Lord, confess that He is your new boss, and commit to listening for what His plan is for your life.

Believe that God has the power to bring life from the dead.

CHAPTER SIX

Inexhaustible Grace

For I am the least of the apostles, and not fit to be called an apostle, because I persecuted the church of God. But by the grace of God I am what I am, and His grace toward me did not prove vain; but I labored even more than all of them, yet not I, but the grace of God with me. — **1 Corinthians 15:9-10, NASB**

Paul was a rabbi among rabbis, given direct authority from the chief priest to go find anyone who believed Jesus was the way, the truth, and the life. He had the power to bind them up and throw them in prison. Paul was the one standing at Steven's feet, commissioning his death.

This was Paul's mission in life—to kill Christians. But God intervened, transformed Paul's heart, and saved him from his wretchedness. Paul acknowledged this, saying, "but by the grace of God, I am what I am and his grace towards me was not in vain; but I labored more abundantly than they all, yet not I but the grace of God that was in me" (1 Corinthians 15:10, NASB).

The Amazing Grace of God

Grace is unmerited favor, something that's inexhaustible. It's more than just forgiveness of sins. It's more than having an undeserved "lucky day." It's something that is so vast and so big that Paul said it was *only* by the grace of God that he was who he was. Paul wasn't making excuses for his shortcomings; he was giving the reason why he was so awesome.

The grace of God turns wimps into warriors, and sinners into saints. Grace leads to good things, not bad things. What Paul was communicating was, "I've turned the world upside down. I have changed lives for the better. I have healed the sick, and I have set free those who were oppressed by the devil. And the reason why I am so famous, if you will, is only by the grace of God." Paul also knew the grace God had extended to him was not in vain.

When I was twelve years old, my parents bought what looked to me like a spaceship. This in-home workout system had a logo on the side: Bowflex. It was ours for twenty-four easy payments of $149.99. This "spaceship" turned into the most expensive clothes hanger the world has ever seen.

Paying a hefty price for something should bring hefty results. You expect to get your money's worth. Paul knew he was the undeserved recipient of the grace of God, and that Jesus "paid a hefty price." He questioned whether God was "getting His money's worth" out of him.

Our job as believers is to run the race with such perseverance that when we cross the line from life to eternity, we should be panting. Paul gave his life for Christ, and he wasn't afraid to say it.

Could you imagine participating in a pastor's meeting and hearing one pastor stand up and say, "Hi, I am Tommy, and I have done more than all of you"? People would think the pastor was arrogant or mentally unstable! But this was what Paul said. Paul knew everything he did was only by the grace of God, and though he had been freely given all things, not everyone uses them.

God gave you the most wonderful gift of grace, but then He puts you to work to do something with that gift that you have been given. The grace of God has appeared to all men, but each of us needs to do something with that grace so that it was not given in vain.

> *And the Word was made flesh, and dwelt among us, (and we beheld his glory, the glory as of the only begotten of the Father), full of grace and truth. John bared witness of him, and cried, saying, "This was he of whom I spake, He that cometh after me is preferred before me: for he was before me. And of his fullness have all we received, and grace for grace. For the law was given by Moses, but grace and truth came by Jesus Christ."* — ***John 1:14-17, KJV***

John said we received "grace for grace." There is an inexhaustible supply of God's unmerited favor. It is something you can never run out of, and it is sufficient. Grace is also intimate and personal. It is conscientious and it is deliberate, and it results in growth. The apostle

Peter even exhorted Christians to grow in grace (2 Peter 3:18).

Paul's mantra was that "to live is Christ and to die is gain" (Philippians 1:21, NASB). Paul knew his life on earth was important, and he labored so much that the world benefited from his existence.

Who Profits from Your Existence?

Paul knew he was the least of all of Christ's apostles. He was well aware that he had been outside of the grace of God, persecuting the Christian church and killing the saints. But by the grace of God, Paul was able to say, "I am what I am, and His grace toward me did not prove vain; but I labored even more than all of them, yet not I, but the grace of God with me" (1 Corinthians 15:10, NASB).

Let's look at Paul's life for a moment. Paul wrote two-thirds of the New Testament. He performed what the Bible calls extraordinary miracles. Paul possessed so much power by the grace of God that people were healed simply because he said so.

So, saying as Paul said, "I am who I am," demands a very clear understanding of *who you actually are.* You are who you are *only* by the grace of God. You are the righteousness of God in Christ Jesus, by the grace of God. You will do greater works than these *because of the grace of God.*

But there must be deliberate involvement. "If any of you wants to be my follower," Jesus said, "you must turn from your selfish ways, take up your cross daily, and follow me" (Luke 9:23, NLT). Jesus calls those who have received this amazing grace to deny themselves. Put aside personal wants and desires, and keep moving forward.

Grace saved Paul, grace kept Paul, grace grew Paul, and grace enabled Paul. Twelve simple men without cell phones, without social media, and without email turned the world upside down because of grace. Clearly, the grace of God is capable and sufficient to reach a lost world for Christ.

God's Grace Is Not in Vain

The fact that Paul was able to say God's grace was not in vain means Paul accomplished his intended purpose. One concordance defines "in vain" as "without a return." God's grace towards Paul, and thus His grace to you and me, is not without a return. It will accomplish something!

If someone asked, "Do you work hard as a Christian?" what would your response be? Probably something similar to: "Well, no, because God does all the work." That's false humility, and it's sinful. Paul would answer, "Look at my back, do you see my scars? Look at these hands; look at these feet. I haven't stopped walking for years. I've been in prison, I've been beaten, I've been jailed, and I've been stoned. You name it I've gone through it." If Paul had worked any harder, he would have been dead.

Your life on this earth as a follower of Jesus will not be all sunshine and rainbows. He sent you here for a purpose. You were called to love.

Our calling as Christians is to take what God gave us freely, and freely give it to the world by giving our lives. The Bible teaches clearly that some people will have works on their record when they get to heaven, but some people will have none. Those with none will still be saved, but only as one through the fire. This means nothing was done with the gift of grace they received. Jesus, the Son of Man, came to seek and save that which was lost and now lives in us. He is our co-laborer. But there will be labor. There will be sacrifice.

Your life on this earth as a follower of Jesus will not be all sunshine and rainbows. He sent you here for a purpose. You were called to love. You were not born in vain, and you were not saved to sit and watch others do the work of the gospel. You are to take part in this great task!

The apostle Peter wrote to the Christians scattered throughout the Roman Empire in the first century, saying, "You therefore, beloved, knowing this beforehand, be on your guard so that you are not carried away by the error of unprincipled men and fall from your own steadfastness" (2 Peter 3:17, NIV).

Peter knew that one day the world would come to an end, and everyone would have to stand before the judgment seat of Christ. Since we know people will face judgment, turn them to Christ!

Many people are afraid to step forward in this profound place of grace. But people won't experience God's grace until they put aside their own strength and hold on to His. And His strength is enough.

> *My grace is sufficient for you, for power is perfected in weakness.* — **2 Corinthians 12:9, NASB**

Paul would rather boast about his weaknesses so the power of Christ would dwell in him. Where there is lack, the grace of God takes over. For the people of God to experience the true grace of God, and to grow in this grace, they must step out of their comfort zone and allow God to stretch them limitations.

Letters Written on Our Hearts

> *Are we beginning to commend ourselves again? Or do we need, as some, letters of commendation to you or from you? You are our letter, written in our hearts, known and read by all men; being manifested that you are a letter of Christ, cared for by us, written not with ink but with the Spirit of the living God, not on tablets of stone but on tablets of human hearts.* — **2 Corinthians 3:1-3, NASB**

Paul was secure in himself and what he had accomplished, and because of this, he didn't need anyone to affirm him.

Our labor for Christ should be visible, or "read" by everyone. Paul was able to speak so highly of himself, without feeling self-righteous, because he knew that he had grown in the grace of God alone and laid hold of everything that God had given to him. And he knew that God's favor was upon him:

> *As God's co-workers we urge you not to receive God's grace in vain. For he says, "In the time of my favor I heard you, and in the day of salvation I helped you." I tell you, now is the time of God's favor, now is the day of salvation.* — **2 Corinthians 6:1-2, NIV**

Your life, the life that God paid for you to have, is the greatest gift that you can ever pass on to others. Run with the gift God has given you, and give others your life. Today is the day that you have been made new in Christ—the day you decide to accomplish your purpose.

The Bible says God created His people for good works before the foundations of the world. You don't *have* to do good works; but it's what you are created to do.

The church is the only body on the face of the planet that has what it takes to change the mess that the world is in.

You are completely capable and have been given everything that you need to make a difference. The next time you look at your little nieces and nephews and your sons and daughters, be reminded that the world needs to be changed *for them.* Give your life so that they have a place to live that is full of love, peace, happiness, and joy because you serve the Prince of Peace. God desires that none shall perish, so why do they?

Once your soul has been saved by the grace of God, there awaits a different type of judgment called the "Judgment Seat of Christ," that is nothing short of a divine awards banquet. The Lord Himself will show you all the things you accomplished for Him.

Paul said in 1 Corinthians 3 that we are God's fellow workers, His field, His building. We are to lay the foundation, which is Christ, and another is to build on it. If a person's foundation is on anything other than Christ, it won't last.

Once your soul has been saved by the grace of God, there awaits a different type of judgment, called the "Judgment Seat of Christ," that is nothing short of a divine awards banquet. The Lord Himself will show you all the things you accomplished for Him.

God will say, "This is what I had planned for you, and this is what you accomplished." Don't miss out on the "well done" from Jesus. God commissioned you to change the world for His name.

CHAPTER SEVEN

No Turning Back

For we are His workmanship, created in Christ Jesus for good works, which God prepared beforehand so that we would walk in them. — ***Ephesians 2: 10, NASB***

Jesus went to Nazareth on the Sabbath day, as was His custom, to the synagogue. He stood up to read from the scroll of the prophet Isaiah that was handed to Him. The book of Luke records the passage Jesus read, a section of Isaiah that the Pharisees knew was speaking of the Messiah:

Unrolling it, he found the place where it is written: "The Spirit of the Lord is on me, because he has anointed me to proclaim good news to the poor. He has sent me to proclaim freedom for the prisoners and recovery of sight for the blind, to set the oppressed free, to proclaim the year of the Lord's favor."l— ***Luke 4:17-19, NASB***

As Jesus finished reading, He closed the scroll and said something profound: "Today this scripture is fulfilled in your hearing" (Luke 4:21, NASB).

This would be equivalent to a pastor reading a part of the Bible that clearly talked about Jesus and telling everyone who was listening, "That was written about me." It was one the boldest things Jesus did in their presence: He was telling these religious leaders that Scripture was being fulfilled in their hearing *at that moment*.

Jesus was saying it was He who was sent to proclaim liberty to the captives and recover sight for the blind. Being in "captivity" refers to a person's repeated return to sinful cycles. It encompasses those things that a person may hate to do but keeps on doing. People may know these things are wrong, but they are bound by them. This could be thought processes or knee-jerk reactions to certain things because of what a person has been through.

For some people, addictive behavior keeps them in bondage. Captivity and addictions are things people cannot control on their own. Jesus wanted to free people from this place of captivity.

Jesus was also sent to recover sight to the blind, but not just natural sight. He was sent to give those who are spiritually lost the ability to see as He sees.

Rich in Mercy Because of His Great Love

But God, being rich in mercy, because of His great love with which He loved us, even when we were dead in our transgressions, made us alive together with Christ (by grace you have been saved), and raised us up with Him, and seated us with Him in the heavenly places in Christ Jesus, so that in the ages to come He might show the surpassing riches of His grace in kindness toward us in Christ Jesus. For by grace you have been saved through faith; and that not of yourselves, it is the gift of God; not as a result of works, so that no one may boast. For we are His workmanship, created in Christ Jesus for good works, which God prepared beforehand so that we would walk in them. — ***Ephesians 2:4-10, NASB***

This passage in Ephesians declares the believer in Christ "His workmanship." Other translations call us His "handiwork." That's another way of saying we are God's masterpiece, the best thing that He ever created. When God says we are His workmanship, created for good works, He didn't mean the times when we happen to do good things. Adam's value was assigned before he took his first steps or spoke his first words. These words in their original Greek language literally mean, "an excellent or an elevated enterprise," or that your existence was supposed to be supernatural. We are His workmanship *always*.

"Created in Christ Jesus for good works" means to live an outstanding, excellent, and elevated life. It means from the time your feet hit the floor in the morning, until you go to bed at night, you are supposed to be supernatural.

But it's important to understand what "supernatural" actually means: it refers to something that is explainable only by God. Your life every day, all day, in everything that you do, was called to show everybody who God is, because you have been called to an elevated existence.

God prepared special works for His people "beforehand." This means He laid the specifics of what you would be doing for Him while on this earth before the foundation of the world. This is His design, and He longs to see you live it out.

But notice, Paul says these works were created "so that we would walk in them." These words translated literally say "make due use of the opportunity to do so." This means you may have to get out of the boat and listen.

Jesus trusted His Father and God's supernatural provisions so much that He willingly laid down His life for the world. Jesus was completely dead for three days, trusting that the Father would raise him to life again. That is true faith.

Awesome for the Kingdom

As Christians, we not only are God's masterpiece but also, as His masterpiece, have an important part in the Kingdom of Heaven. We are awesome because God has provided salvation by grace, through faith. We are awesome because He has made us awesome. We are certainly not awesome because we've earned it!

When Jesus called you, He knew beforehand what He called you to: "Not that I have already obtained it or have already arrived at my goal, but I press on to take hold of that for which Christ Jesus took hold of me" (Philippians 3:12, NIV).

Paul says he presses on to grab hold of what God had already prepared for him. "Press on" literally means the flexing of every muscle in your body, something that you actually can't do on your own. It is with such tenacity and momentum that every muscle from head to toe flexes. That's the effort that Paul put into attaining what God prepared for him.

When Jesus calls you to do something, honor Him by stepping out in faith. You may not be able to do it without Him (mostly likely you won't!), but because you believe in Him, walk boldly into the circumstance that is far, far out of your reality. Paul knew God had a specific destiny for him, and he was going to do everything to attain it.

Believers often say their lives are much harder once they become a follower of Jesus. The truth is, it's not easy following Christ. Paul acknowledged his own difficulties, but pressed on in spite of them. Like him, we too have to make the decision to persevere when trials occur.

When Jesus walked up to a motley group of fisherman on the shores of the Sea of Galilee and said, "Follow me," their response was active. These men followed Jesus unabashedly, and faithfully made a decision that they were never going to turn back, even if things became rough.

Believers often say their lives are much harder once they become a follower of Jesus. The truth is, it's not easy following Christ. Paul acknowledged his own difficulties, but pressed on in spite of them. Like him, we too have to make the decision to persevere when trials occur.

In Philippians 3:14, Paul says, "With this goal in mind, I strive toward the prize of the upward call of God in Christ Jesus. And I press towards the goals for the price of the upward call of God in Christ Jesus" (NASB).

The phrase "upward call" includes the same two words used for good works: *elevated existence.* God's call is an invitation upward, to a heavenly home. These words echo Jesus' promise that His departure was good because He was going "to prepare a place" for His followers (John 14:3, NIV).

Jesus promised He would "come back and take you to be with me that you also may be where I am" (John 14:3, NIV). Jesus has already called you and me to live in that heavenly place.

And so Paul flexed every muscle in his spiritual body to ensure that he would attain the heavenly reality that Jesus called him to. He knew that looking back would cause him to stop moving forward.

Four Things to Forget

1. **Your Failures**

Past failures give no indication of what God desires to do for you and through you in the future. Paul was on his way to kill Christians when he was converted, yet God used him in miraculous ways.

> *For I will forgive their wickedness and will remember their sins no more. By calling this covenant "new," he has made the first one obsolete; and what is obsolete and outdated will soon disappear. —* ***Hebrews 8:12-13, NIV***

Paul could have allowed his past failures to consume him based on the law. But this would have prevented him from being what God intended. The law demanded perfection, guaranteeing our failure; God's grace supplied perfection, guaranteeing our prosperity. If you want to live a truly free life, it's important to distinguish the covenants properly. Jesus did away with the old covenant, making it obsolete. Our past failures are now seen through the filter of the death and resurrection of Christ.

The hardest things for people to forget are their failures. But God desires to remove them forever. He called this covenant “new” for a reason. Every person who existed before the death of Jesus was defined and labeled by what they accomplished. They had to follow the Law in order to be considered righteous by God, but everybody failed. But God loved His people so much that He sent his Son to pay for the sin of the entire world.

Now, Christians have the law written on their heart, giving us the ability to keep the Law in a way never before possible.

What determines a person’s righteousness is the honor that is given to Jesus’ sacrifice. Do you believe Jesus paid for your sin? If you do, you are forgiven and have Jesus written on your heart.

2. **Unanswered Prayers**

Many people feel far from God because prayers have gone unanswered. Someone isn’t being healed, a marriage continues to fall apart, or a child continues to rebel.

Elisha prayed for rain seven times. The first time he prayed for rain, he told the servant to go and check. The servant came back and said, “There is nothing.” Many people would conclude they weren’t supposed to be praying for rain. Elisha knelt a second time and said, “God, let it rain! We’ve been in the drought for three years.” Again, he sent his servant to check, but still no rain. Then a third time, fourth time, fifth time, and sixth time, Elisha said to the servant, “Go check.”

Elisha had such conviction and faith in what God said He was going to do that he refused to give up on the promise. True faith is immovable and unshakeable because it's founded on the Word of God. If God says there are promises to inherit, press on to ensure that you lay hold of those promises.

The seventh time Elisha sent the servant out, he returned saying, "I see a cloud, and it's *huge*!"

And the rain came.

Forget unanswered prayers. Keep praying as if it is the first time you've prayed for that specific request. God will answer.

3. **Forget Hidden Sin**

People hide sin because they don't believe Jesus can take care of it. It's not because they love sin or want to continue in it. It's because deep down they believe they can take care of sin on their own, just as Adam and Eve covered their nakedness with a fig leaf. Accept Jesus' sacrifice, receive forgiveness, and then forget about past sin. It has been taken care of.

4. **Forget about Past Victories**

Paul converted entire towns, planted churches, and trained pastors, but that wasn't enough for him. He pressed on for more. He didn't camp on his previous victories. When too much emphasis is put on victories in ministry, people become complacent, thinking they have attained all God has desired to accomplish through them.

Forget about victories, because you didn't accomplish them, anyway! They can cause a person to become stuck in the past. If you are living for past accomplishments, know that Jesus has already moved on to the next stage of your life and it's time for you to catch up.

What you see as success in life is only the beginning of the glorious existence God has called you to. Paul planted churches and moved on. No victory caused him to let go of the next one ahead. The Bible says that those who are righteous are "planted in the house of the *LORD*, they will flourish in the courts of our God. They will still bear fruit in old age; they will stay fresh and green…" (Psalm 92:13-14, NIV).

You have much fruit to bear ahead!

An Irrevocable Calling

Paul, speaking of Israel and the promises God made to the nation for land and blessing, said, "the gifts and the calling of God are irrevocable" (Romans 11:29, ESV). The King James Version translates this phrase as "without repentance." These God-given promises can never be revoked.

The definition of a gift is "the favor that you receive without any merit of your own." The gifts of divine grace, faith, knowledge, healing, holiness, and virtue are all gifts that are irrevocable in God's economy.

Lastly, the word "calling" means "an excellent existence," or "an upward call." Paul knew that the gifts

God gave him and the calling on his life could never be taken away.

This promise is for you, too.

Don't be ashamed to claim the truth that you are the righteousness of God in Christ Jesus. You are forgiven, faultless and redeemed.

But people need encouragement that the gift of God is in them. Paul instructed Timothy: "For this reason I remind you to fan into flame the gift of God, which is in you through the laying on of my hands" (2 Timothy 1:6, NIV). He also reminded Timothy that "God has not given us a spirit of fear, but of power and of love and of a sound mind" (2 Timothy 1:7, KJV). Knowing it's hard for some people to accept what Christ has done, we must combat this fear or doubt.

Don't be ashamed to claim the truth that you are the righteousness of God in Christ Jesus. You are forgiven, faultless and redeemed. Don't be ashamed to say that you are awesome and that you have an excellent existence!

Claim with boldness the testimony of our Lord because He bought, purchased, and paid for everything you need when He died on the cross. More importantly, don't be ashamed to live your life based on His gifts.

If you are living in fear, remember: God didn't give you that spirit. He gave you a spirit of power, a sound mind, and a steady heart. You are founded on a Rock that's unmovable and strong. There is a world of lost people, who will only be saved when the body of Christ unites and is not ashamed of the testimony of God. Knowing and believing these things will result in miracles for the Kingdom.

Step Out of the Boat

Matthew 14:22-33 tells the story of one disciple's experience with the supernatural. Jesus' disciples were out on a boat in the Sea of Galilee. They looked across the water to see what they thought was a ghost. Jesus greeted them, saying, "Be of good cheer, it is I, Jesus."

Peter was unsure it was the Lord, and responded, "Jesus, if it's you, bid me to come." Peter was asking for Jesus to call him to a supernatural existence. Jesus beckoned to Peter, "It is I, come." Peter stepped out of the boat and miraculously walked on the water toward Jesus, until he took his eyes off his Master. Peter immediately grew fearful and began to sink. Notice, it says "began," as if the sinking never actually occurred, but only began.

There was nothing supernatural about Peter sinking below the water, I'm sure it looked just like you or I when we sink. Immediately, Jesus reached His hand out and grabbed him, and rescued him.

Have you ever wondered how Peter was able to get back to the boat? The Word says that when Jesus *and* Peter returned to the boat, Jesus, God in the flesh, laid hold of him and Peter experienced the supernatural. You don't think Jesus jumped in and started swimming, do you? This is the God we serve: He lives in the impossible and guarantees that we can live the same life. Step out in faith to that supernatural existence! You might stumble along the way, but the God of creation will stretch out His hand and hold on to you.

This is the gospel; this is the life you've been called to.

You have been called to live a supernatural life that daily walks on water. Forget your failures, fears, hidden sins, and even victories. Today is the day when you are going to step out of the boat and say: "I can't do this on my own." You don't need to try harder. Simply make a declaration that you're not going to turn around, but you are going to step out into the impossible, into joy unspeakable, and into a peace beyond understanding.

And when you fall, Jesus will catch you.

This is the *Famous Church*. Now, go and be it!

About the Author

Tommy Miller is the lead pastor of Legacy Church in New Philadelphia, Ohio. He is a husband, father, speaker, and is in love with knowing Jesus and making Him known.

About SermonToBook.Com

SermonToBook.com began with a simple belief: that sermons should be touching lives, *not* collecting dust. That's why we turn sermons into high-quality books that are accessible to people all over the globe.

Turning your sermon or sermon series into a book exposes more people to God's Word, better equips you for counseling, adds credibility to your ministry, and even helps make ends meet during tight times.

John 21:25 tells us that the world itself couldn't contain the books that would be written about the work of Jesus Christ. Our mission is to try anyway. Because, in Heaven, there will no longer be a need for sermons or books. Our time is now.

If God so leads you, we'd love to work with you on your sermon or sermon series.

Visit www.sermontobook.com to learn more.

Made in the USA
Columbia, SC
23 June 2017